Boss Up, Beautiful!

I0149187

Boss Up, Beautiful!

Boss Up, Beautiful!

Owning the Power of Your Intuition as a Female Entrepreneur

Amber Millman

Boss Up, Beautiful!

Copyright © 2018 Amber Millman/Amber Millman, LLC

Cover Design © Shawna Poliziani/ShawnaPoliz Design
email hello@shawnapoliziani.com

ISBN-13: 978-0-692-68460-3
ISBN-10: 0692684603

For more, visit www.AmberMillman.com
or email info@ambermillman.com

To my family, for always supporting me on all my
crazy endeavors.
Thank you.
I love you.

Boss Up, Beautiful!

To Boss Up:

Take ownership of ones' life, by directing the full
capacity of their time, resources, and attention
toward a specific goal, or intent. In other words:
step up, raise your standards, up your game, and
take responsibility for the direction of your life and
the full maturity of your dreams.[1]

---

[1] Source:
https://www.urbandictionary.com/define.php?term=Boss-Up

CONTENTS

Connect with Amber

www.AmberMillman.com
Instagram: @ambermillman

"Life is dance between making it happen
And letting it happen."
Arianna Huffington

INTRODUCTION
Who am I?

I'm Amber Millman and I've been an entrepreneur for the past thirteen years. In this book the chapters are filled with my story, my "failures" (which I like to call lessons), and my successes. I've relied on my intuition to guide me, and I want this book to encourage you to own your intuition and make the change or changes that you feel deep down in your gut need to be made. And if you truly know they need to be made, I'm here to tell you that it doesn't matter how old you are, or what else is going on in your life, the time is now to own your power.

This book is also about letting you know that no matter where you come from, it does not dictate where you are going! I didn't go to Wharton

School of Business or Harvard Business School and I honestly never really created a formal business plan. I just made decisions for my business based on my intuition. I followed my intuition, researched and worked hard!

I want you to believe in yourself and believe that you can do anything you choose to. Whether that's first starting out in business, starting over, writing that book, or ridding yourself of toxic relationships. No matter what it is, choose you, choose your happiness and no matter what follow your intuition!

I want you to believe that if I can do it, you can do it too! I want you to push the boundaries of your comfort zone. I want you to take risks and embrace who you are and be confident choosing the path for your unique journey. Your hopes and dreams are worth fighting for and they're worth the lessons you will learn because you'll use them going forward. I'm not going to say it's easy but what I will tell you is, it sure is worth it!

You totally got this, beautiful! Now let's go!

"I think of myself as somebody who from an early age knew I was responsible for myself, and I had to make good."
Oprah Winfrey

CHAPTER ONE
Humble Beginnings

I've been an entrepreneur for as long as I can remember. If I'm being completely honest I was about 17 years old when I knew I wanted to be one. That year, my childhood home went up for auction. It had been abandoned by my parents who divorced when I was eleven years old. Once I heard about this auction, I told my mother and father to sign the house over to me and I would make the payment arrangements with the city for the back taxes. And that's what I did. I saw the value in fixing and flipping it and I wanted to try. However, being a teen mom on public assistance, attending school and only bringing in part-time income from my job at Dunkin Donuts, I couldn't keep up with the payments (plus the house needed a lot of work that I couldn't afford). So unfortunately, I lost the house. I felt like a complete failure, but I dusted myself off and acknowledged that it wasn't my time. Once I was finished with high school, I immediately enrolled in to my local community college. I started out slowly because I wasn't sure how I'd be able to balance being a mother and a college student. Once I was in college for a couple of semesters it taught me the structure and discipline I needed.

After I found my balance and felt like I was established I applied for my first real job at a top law firm in Philadelphia. I was super nervous walking into such a formal work place, but I just knew that's exactly where I belonged at that time. I breezed through the interview and I got the job!

I finally felt proud of myself and I felt like I was moving in the right direction. I was able to go to school, work a part-time job and take care of my child. This is what ignited me, and I just kept on making goals and achieving them.

I knew that I wanted to buy a home back when I was seventeen; I don't know why but I would dream of the day that I could purchase a home. I suppose I was looking for stability on my own terms after renting an apartment for two years. Real estate always intrigued me, and I knew one day that I wanted to be a real estate investor so purchasing a home would be an asset and the beginning of my real estate investing dream.

During my last semester in school, I decided that I wanted to buy a house with my fiancé. So, I asked my employer to make me a full time legal assistant, so I could make it happen. I was twenty years old at this point and my son was about to enter kindergarten that fall so I wanted to make sure I had a permanent place for him to grow up. A place that we could all call HOME. I wanted to not only be a good mother, but I wanted to be a positive role model for him and to show him that if you set goals and work towards them every day you can achieve anything.

In the spring I finally finished my schooling and received my Associates Degree in Business, at this point I owned my home for six months and I was working full time as a legal assistant at one of the top law firms in my industry. I felt like a success, like I beat the odds and I felt completely confident that I could do anything I wanted to. It's like once I had the taste of success or maybe I should say fulfillment, I became addicted to testing myself. Setting goals and tackling them. I definitely wasn't like the rest of my peers. Sometimes I thought I sounded crazy for dreaming so big and having such confidence. I just had this feeling since I was seventeen (even after having my son as a teen) that I was meant for more. More what, I didn't know exactly, but just more. Maybe it was just that it made me feel incredibly happy at that time in my life because I was proving to myself that I was not just another statistic. I was proud of myself.

After I was out of school and working full-time for a few years I started to become bored in my current position at the law firm (I call it the three-year itch, but I'll get into that later in the book!) I started looking for other job opportunities. I landed a new job making a good salary and was thrilled for the change. A month into my new job, I found out that my fiancé and I were pregnant with my second child. Since my first child was now 8 years old, I had a career and my life was stable, I felt that I was ready to be a mother again.

Once my second son was born, I quickly realized that I did not want to go back to work, but really had no choice. That's when the entrepreneurial bug bit me once more. An inner voice told me I needed to make a change. I knew at the age of 24 that there was no way I could allow a job to dictate my life. I became obsessed in trying to find a way out of the corporate world.

In June of 2004, my fiancé and I eloped and upon my return I was "fired" for calling out the day I was supposed to return. My flight was delayed, and I was just extremely tired. Now could I have made my way into the office? Yes, but I also knew that the company I was working for was closing by the end of the year, so I was not exactly committed at this point, if I'm being completely honest. All I had on my mind was figuring out exactly what I could do to earn money and stay home with my kids. So that's what I did: I stayed home for a while and figured out what I wanted to do next.

I always had dreams of flipping real estate. So that's what I did. I started studying, reading and learning different real estate investing techniques. I found a couple properties and lined them up with a buyer. I made a little money and put it in the bank until I knew what my next move would be. And since it was not a huge amount of money and I didn't really know what I wanted to invest it in, I decided to go back to work as a paralegal until my next big idea or opportunity came to me. This way, I could save the money I made from my real estate investing and still bring in a paycheck on a weekly basis. My day job was my insurance.

By the time I was 28 years old, I was completely desperate to get out of corporate America. I was so tired of the same routine day in and day out and I was tired of being away from my children for such a long period of the day. It started to feel like it was Groundhog Day and I could not stand asking permission for time off. I overall hated not being in control of my own life.

I had a few people telling me what I should do with my money and then one day I decided to invest in a business that was more aligned with my life at that time, which was a mother with two children ages twelve and three. Since I had young children, I knew I didn't want to work weekends or evenings. I actually knew that from the time I was sixteen working at Dunkin Donuts and was scheduled to work on Christmas Day from 12 pm to 6 pm. My oldest son was just a baby at the time but leaving him on that day just hurt my soul. It didn't feel right to me (there's that intuition again). So, I made a pros and cons list and proceeded from there. It was all very analytical. I just based it on whether I could provide a decent income with the hours that worked for me and my family. It sounded like a good idea, so I jumped in, and I mean jumped! Full steam ahead, per usual.

The business that I decided to invest in was a day care center for children. It really worked at this point in my life. I was a mother of two boys, ages twelve and three. I thought: perfect - no working weekends, set hours of operation, I can take my children along with me, etc.

The first couple years were pretty good; I think the most exciting part for me was the fact that I was creating something. Something new and fresh and I was learning again and stimulating my mind, incorporating everything I learned from school and my corporate job and infusing it into this new business. But, unfortunately, the novelty wore off. When things weren't going so well, it was horrible. I didn't have that fighting spirit for it, you know? The one you have when you're really into something, that passion? Yeah, that wasn't there, and I'd often wonder to myself: what did I get myself into? That's when I knew, I knew I wanted out. I just didn't know how to get out and I was afraid. For the first time in my entrepreneurial journey, I was scared. I didn't have an escape plan, so I felt trapped. Trapped in a business where I was responsible for six to eight staff members and thirty children and their families. It was a huge weight for someone my age. All I wanted to do at this point was focus on my own family and it sucked, BIG TIME!

I didn't realize the demand and the toll this business would take on me. When you're responsible for thirty children and eight staff members on a daily basis it becomes quite grueling.

I suppose the glory wore off after a few years because of course my children got older and I moved to a neighboring state to get my children out of the city and into a better school system. Most importantly I wasn't passionate about the business anymore. I stayed in it for a couple more years but just couldn't do it much longer. I was starting to feel depressed because the thought of taking care of other people's children while my children were growing and changing was really starting to overwhelm me. It just wasn't making me happy and I was telling myself I was being ungrateful. I learned a valuable lesson here: if you don't love it, the money will not matter! I had to make a change. I only want to do things I'm excited about. I only want to invest my time and money in things that make me happy.

Looking back, I've always been a person who works and provides for myself. I started at the age of thirteen knocking on doors and asking people to subscribe to *The Philadelphia Inquirer*, the daily newspaper in my hometown. At the age of sixteen I wanted to get back to work however, there weren't too many jobs for 16-year-old back in the '90s, but I landed a job at Dunkin' Donuts. From there, I decided it was time to go back to school and enroll in college. And then by the time I was eighteen, I landed my first "legit" job as a file clerk in a big

Center City law firm. Within a year I was promoted to legal assistant. I worked as a legal assistant/paralegal for eight years before leaving the industry for good to be a full-time entrepreneur.

I have been super ambitious all my life. I became a mother at 16, which forced me to grow up really, really fast. I realized early on that I needed to continue my education so that I could provide for my son. I think that most type A personalities are created from people who have struggles whether as an adult or as children. They then have this drive to never feel helpless or less-than again.

I suppose the one thing about growing up poor is knowing that you can make it through no matter what. Everything else is just a bonus. I honestly think that when you come from a place of not really having money, you become stronger and fiercer in the way you go after what you want. There's a sense of fearlessness within you because you already know what it's like to go without. You're much more willing to gamble on yourself and bank on yourself because in all reality what do you really have to lose?

All my struggles, all of my sacrifices and all of my success were so my children would know that they could be anything and do anything they want in life, no matter what. They were my driving force.

It was to prove to them that, you can beat the odds no matter what.

It's time to Boss Up!

I want you to list three accomplishments you achieved.

1.
2.
3.

Now I want you to explain how accomplishing these things made you feel.

Boss Notes

What did you learn most from this chapter?

"You own everything that happened to you. Tell your stories. If people wanted you to write warmly about them, they should have behaved better."
Anne Lamott

CHAPTER TWO
Crossroads

Here I was, thirty-six years old, an entrepreneur, and at a total crossroads in my life. I was no longer passionate about my business and had no idea what to do next. Every decision I made up until this point was based on whether or not it was good for my family. And, honestly, pure faith that anything I did, would be successful. I don't know, I just had this undeniable confidence in myself. But that confidence seemed to be waning. I would question myself and why I wasn't making a move to change my situation. Was it because I now had more to lose? I mean I did have two children, two homes, and a car loan. You get what I'm saying. Was I afraid that my next venture would result in failure? Sure. A person can't be lucky all the time, right? Oh, boy, the fear was real! That shit can keep you seriously paralyzed.

However, I learned valuable lessons as an entrepreneur. First and foremost, always follow your intuition in business (and in life in general). If you are worried and have the feeling that something just isn't quite right, listen to your intuitive voice and just follow your heart. You'll save yourself a lot of time, money and heartache. That's one of the biggest lessons I've learned in business. I've had to learn this lesson not once, but a couple times in my thirteen years of entrepreneurship. As Oprah says, "You will continue to be tested until you learn the lesson." And, Oprah, I've learned the lesson! It has been duly noted!

Now I'm not saying feel sorry for me at all because I've learned so much by being an entrepreneur. Not only did I make an income, but I made an income while obtaining my real-life MBA in business. The ups and the downs of my experience all gave me valuable insight and lessons.

Being an entrepreneur is not for the faint of heart; at times it can be an absolute mental roller coaster and you must be prepared. You have payroll to meet, taxes to pay, supplies to order, rent to pay, licenses and permits to maintain, and the list goes on. You have got to wear so many hats in one day and it can be especially hard as a mother and a wife. Because, ultimately, it's not just your livelihood on the line, it's that of your employees and your family.

For three long years (2012-2015), I battled with myself on whether or not I should close my business. I was completely stressed out, unmotivated, anxious and slightly depressed. I didn't even recognize the person I was anymore. Depression is a serious thing, and it can completely stifle you. I would often sit and wonder how I could feel this way. I would tell myself I was being ungrateful, selfish and unappreciative of the fact that I had a business that gave me a decent income. But as the old saying goes, money doesn't buy you happiness.

I was stressed because there were day care centers popping up on every corner. The area where my center was located was on the decline and I felt like it was no longer ideal for me. There was a shooting just one block down from my location, across from a public library. Prior to that, there was a gas leak and subsequent explosion one block down in the opposite direction, which resulted in a fatality. The explosion was directly across the street from another day care center and I remember it really shaking me to my core. Between the shooting and the gas explosion, it opened my eyes to how much I was responsible for. I had to worry about the welfare of these children and my staff members on a daily basis. The weight just became too heavy, knowing that something completely out of my control could happen yet I would feel so responsible and devastated.

There was also a period in my business when I went through an upsetting incident. I had to let go of a "friend" from my place of business because she just wasn't pulling her weight. It was a long time coming. I would have people coming to me and telling me she wasn't doing her job. On top of that, I felt deep down she wasn't doing her job to her full capability. It wasn't just people at the place of business complaining about how she would conduct herself but mutual "friends" would also come to me and tell me about her behavior behind the scenes. It was such a hard decision for me, but it absolutely had to be done. Once I did that, within a week her true colors were shown. I was then bullied by her and a middle aged male figure in her family. They were bullying me via the internet, and just saying the most disgusting vile things. I was never ever going to stoop to that level, so I decided, I decided right then and there to just fight for what was right, and then, let go in peace.

These people were most certainly not acting like adults, they were acting like juveniles. As I look back at the history though, this was always their way of doing things. This isn't the first day care center that this man tried to hostilely takeover. If I didn't stand up for myself and take legal action, this would have been his third child care center that he bullied his way into. There's a pattern of this type of behavior from both individuals.

As all of this transpired I had to cut a lot of other people out of my life too because I realized in one of my hardest moments they weren't there for me. In fact, the people I removed from my life were the "mutual friends" that would come to me and tell me things about this "friend", ironic, right? I know now it's because they all had something in common, and that was the same addictions and the same mindset. I saw it for what it was and knew I was not going in the same direction they were.

What I've learned is that friendships shouldn't feel like work. You should definitely have good vibes around them, have similar morals, and have respect for them and respect how they conduct themselves. And If you don't, cut them loose, remove them from your life. Cutting these people out of my life was much needed and I will be forever grateful for this life lesson.

I'd been an entrepreneur for eight years when all this happened and after a lot of the stress I had to start figuring things out. I would often wonder "what's next?" I was a girl that always had a goal. I was a teen mom, so I was always trying to prove something. Go to school! Go to college! Get that secure corporate nine-to-five job! Start that business! Show them, that being a teen mom does not define you! However, after this experience and the betrayals of my supposed "friendships" I started to wonder: what is it that I really want to do? What do I truly enjoy?

Prior to running this business, I was young, ambitious, happy, outgoing, social and most importantly **confident**. But something happened, something shifted: I lost my passion for the work.

At the time, though, fear just kept creeping in. I knew I needed to make a change, but I just didn't know what that was or how to go about doing it. I felt completely and utterly trapped in that business. Fear kept me in the business long past its expiration date because I had a family to support. I am a mother, a wife, a financial contributor and for the first time in my life, I was completely unsure of everything. I knew I had to make a change soon. How could I live a happy life and make the people around me happy if I was completely miserable? I knew I couldn't and that plagued me for a while.

It was June 2014 and I was on vacation with my husband for our ten-year wedding anniversary in Puerto Vallarta, Mexico. Coincidentally or not so coincidentally, we were staying at an all-inclusive resort called Now Amber. Go figure!

It was maybe our second day there and something just came over me while I was sitting on the beach watching the ocean. As I was staring out into the ocean, I can't really explain it, except to call it an epiphany. I finally realized how I wanted to spend my days and ultimately the rest of my life. I knew I didn't want to wait a whole year to take a week off to spend with my loved ones. I wanted to spend my days doing only things that I truly enjoyed, being creative and most importantly being happy. Not just because I was on vacation or because I had something on the calendar to look forward to but because every day I was happy with how I was earning and living my life. Now, don't get me wrong. I know that not every day can be a magical fairy tale, but ultimately realizing life is too short to not be happy in your day-to-day job is just bullshit; it's wasted time and we aren't guaranteed tomorrow.

It was in this moment on the beach in Mexico when I realized that I wanted to live a freer life. That's when I decided on that trip in June 2014 that that would be my last year in my child care center business. I had wanted out for years but that day on the beach in Mexico I realized I had to just let it go. I would ride out the rest of my lease and then when it was up I would not renew. I was just ready to be done. And when the time came in 2015, let me tell you, I was afraid, but I was more afraid of staying in a business that felt like it was sucking the life and happiness out of me.

In hindsight, I noticed that the number eight resurfaces again and again. It is like reinvention after about every eight or so years for me. My children are eight and a half years apart. From the time of the purchase of my first home to my second home is eight and a half years and I closed my business after eight years. I'm starting to see a pattern here. A cycle, so to speak.

My intuitive guide kicks in when it's time for change and you know you just have to take the leap! They don't call it a leap of faith for nothing. Some people are really good at planning and I plan, too, but I also know myself well enough now to know that when it's time to make a move I MOVE, like jump in and figure out how to swim later. That's just how I work. If I don't, I'll be standing on that ledge and teeter back and forth forever.

My business felt like such a burden and it was stunting my growth. I felt shackled to it and I had to break free. My creativity was lying dormant and I just felt the need to spread my wings once again. If I didn't do it then, I would have been stuck in it for another year and that just seemed too long to me. I already spent two years longer in the business than I really wanted to spend. It was time to move on. It no longer fit with my lifestyle. I was changing. My children were getting older. And I realized all I really wanted to do was be myself.

I know this may sound crazy to some, like why would you just shut the business down? My response is, you have to be happy. If you don't have peace of mind and happiness, you have nothing. I'd rather take a chance and ride out the ups and downs of the unknown than to spend one more year in a place I didn't want to be. I knew deep down that I just had to jump and figure it out along the way.

That may not be the answer for everyone but that was the answer for me. I also knew that every time I took a chance on myself before I was OK. Not to say that everything was easy, or everything worked out as planned, but does it ever really work out exactly as planned? No, right? If it did, there would be no excitement and no gratitude for the lessons you're meant to learn. And I truly believe the more you take that leap the more confident you become. You become confident because you know that by taking that chance you are trying to make the difference and the change that you desire in your life. Look, I'm not saying that everything has worked out as planned for me because honestly it hasn't, but what I do know is just because things don't work out as planned or how I thought they would doesn't mean it didn't work out. There's always a lesson to be learned that will make you stronger, smarter and tougher for the next decision or the next task or the next opportunity. All I can say is just follow your heart. You know what you have to do, so don't let fear stop you. You'll regret it if you do. I'll be honest: I have not one regret, not one, for closing my business and that is the truth! I'd rather ride the entrepreneurial roller coaster then sit idle and be miserable.

It's time to Boss Up!

When you are feeling angry or frustrated about a situation or circumstance, I want you to ask yourself some questions.

What is this situation teaching me?

What lesson am I being forced to learn to take with me as I move forward?

Why is this problem coming my way?

Boss Notes

What did you learn most from this chapter?

*"Great people do things before
they're ready."*
Amy Poehler

CHAPTER THREE
Overcoming Fear

I kicked fear in the ass when I decided to close my business for good. I wanted to create a life and business which truly filled me with passion, creativity and true happiness. I overcame my fear by remembering why I started (which was to be a provider and have freedom) and remembering that I was a successful female entrepreneur. I've always been okay before, so why not now? Also, I remembered to believe in myself again.

When I made that decision to close the doors I was finally placing myself first. I was ready to follow my heart and see where it would take me. I was ready to start living the life of my dreams and willing to jump into the unknown.

I want you to know that there may come a time where you no longer feel like a relationship, a client or something that you once enjoyed doing fits with your vision or your plan or your life. That's because we are always (or we should be) evolving and growing. Be open and prepared for change and embrace it, don't fight it. It's okay to change your mind. I know I'm not the same person at age thirty-nine that I was at age twenty-nine. My interests have changed, my desires have changed and quite frankly my priorities have changed.

We already know what we want deep down inside, so why do we wait? Maybe it's because what we want is buried so deep because of all our "adult responsibilities".

It was actually really empowering to have the freedom to take some time to get my thoughts together and my ideas together. I got to focus on my life and my family more.

Things really started to shift for me once I stopped trying to control everything and just followed my inner guide. She is a badass bitch, after all! We've been through many storms together and it's time I hand over the baton. It's like she's talking to me saying, "Move over, bitch! I've got this."

To be completely transparent, nothing made sense during the year of 2016. That's because I was so used to making a plan an executing it however, it seemed like every time I would come up with a plan I'd have a setback. I really learned to let go of trying to control the outcome and let things unfold naturally. Instead of stressing out about something I would rely on the way I felt and then I would react accordingly. It was like my intuition kicked in because I was tired of being so hard on my mind. I was always using my mind and I literally became burnt out I suppose. It's like my intuition is now in the driver's seat and my responses and reactions are in the passenger seat. It's as if my body and mind quite literally are not having it anymore. If I don't feel fired up and have good energy, then I don't do it. My intuition is telling me, "Save it for something that makes you want to scream with excitement!" I was healing, I was awakening, and it felt amazingly beautiful and scary at the same time.

Once day, I was wondering why I seemed to feel anxious every three years or so. That's when I stumbled upon an article on the Internet titled "7 Signs You Might Be a Serial Entrepreneur" by Neil Patel and low and behold I had all the signs. Finally, I knew I wasn't crazy (well, maybe), kidding, but that's a whole other story. The questions are as follows:

"Are you restless after about three or four years?" Yes.

"You are curious and customer-centric?" Yes.

"You have more fear of regret than of failure?" YES!

"You started a business before you could drive?" Well, if you consider me taking over my family home, starting a business, then YES!

"You recognize your current startup won't make money?" Yes, I intuitively know when to walk away!

"You simply know you want to start another company?" Yes, always.

"You already have your hands in two or three businesses?" At least 2-3 business ideas swirling around in my head.

And then it hit me: there's no reason to feel so anxious or feel like I'm crazy. I started to acknowledge the fact that I may just be a *Serial Entrepreneur or a form of it.*

A serial entrepreneur is:

An entrepreneur who continuously comes up with new ideas and starts new businesses. As opposed to a typical entrepreneur, who will often come up with a single idea, start the company, and then see it through, a serial entrepreneur will often come up with the idea and get things started, but then give responsibility to someone else and move on to a new idea and a new venture. This can be a good thing if the individual has lots of unique ideas and is the best one suited to get each one started but can be a bad thing if the individual stops putting time into a company that needs his or her help in order to try to move forward with a new idea that may or may not succeed."[2]

I totally agree with the definition. I'd come up with ideas and wanted to pursue them, but my business at the time just started to require too much of my time or at least it felt that way because that's how resentful I started to become of it.

I knew once I let go, I would find something else that didn't feel like work or at least I wouldn't dread the work that was required. I mean I'm a girl who has built websites, applied for business licenses and zoning, managed employees, overseen construction, balanced a budget and the list goes on. All I really needed to do was hone in on the things that made me happy and do more of them every day and then start implementing all of my business skills.

I truly believe I'm just meant to take all the lessons I learned from those experiences and apply them to one of my best projects yet: my happiness. I

---

[2] Source http://www.businessdictionary.com/definition/serial-entrepreneur.html

had it all backwards. I was so focused on making money that I let my passions fall by the wayside. Oh, those lessons!

Here is a list of things that I actually love and have loved since I was a teenager (but put on the back burner to make money as an adult): reading beauty and fashion/style magazines and looking at the latest trends, listening to music, creating DIY projects, looking at real estate trends, interior design, and talking about business. What are some of the things you like to do that you may have placed on the back burner?

You have to sit down and dig deep. And for Type A personalities, it's hard to sit still but it's absolutely necessary if you want a fulfilling and passion-filled business. Remember that the stillness won't last forever; realize that things will get better. Have someone you trust 100% who will listen when you need to talk.

I also want you to know that fear is normal. It's a natural reaction to change or anything unfamiliar for that matter. The thing is you have to figure out how to move past it. You just have to keep moving, you have to push. You don't have to make big strides everyday day but try to take little steps. We tend to over think, and complicate things based off of fear. In my opinion, action combats fear and anxiety every time. I understood that fear was just in my mind and I want you to realize that too. It was that old saying: *fear is just false evidence appearing real*. So, to combat my anxiety, I decided to focus on me and to focus on what I wanted in my life and business.

As I look back, I realized that I used to be so fearless. Or maybe it's not that I was fearless because to be honest I've always felt fear but was never afraid to proceed anyway. I think I forgot that about myself for a while. I'm starting to see that I've always pushed past fear to get where I wanted to be. I began to get that back. I'm feeling inspired, empowered and motivated on most days or at least excited about my new chapter, which ultimately is me becoming more aware and a better version of myself and helping others do the same! Yeah, I don't know what tomorrow holds because I finally feel like the possibilities are limitless.

As for business, I was building personal relationships and friendships with other like-minded females in the online world. I was starting over. Creating my circle with like-minded people. I was changing and not everyone was going to get it, but that's alright, they didn't have to.

For instance, I was at a friend's 40th birthday party with people I've known for twenty plus years and I had not seen most of these people for a little over a year. When I told one of my old friends that I closed my business, she asked how was I doing? "I'm good," I said. "I'm feeling good." "I knew you wouldn't be down for long," she said.

And I immediately responded: "I've never been down." I'll be honest I was taken aback by her statement because the truth is I never looked at it that way. I never looked at it as me being down just because I closed my business. I don't think she meant it maliciously at all. I just don't know if she knew that I chose to close my business, I choose not to renew the lease, I chose not to renew my licensing, and I most certainly chose not to stay in an unfulfilling, non-passionate business anymore. I chose to believe in my intuition and most importantly, I choose to believe in myself once again. Like I said, I never looked at it as me being down. I looked at it as if I took a jump into the big blue sea of possibilities.

I feel like at this point in the entrepreneurial game I've got a pretty good handle on it. It can be an emotional roller coaster. I guess I'd describe it as driving: you have to know when step on the gas, push the break and when you can relax and enjoy cruise control. Also, I'm at a point where I've driven economy, luxury and even a mac truck. It's pretty much the same, you just have to adjust to the feel of the drive. In business, you start out driving economy, sometimes you drive luxury smooth like butter, and then you master that big mac truck. I have it under control.

I've realized by being a type A personality / Alpha female at such a young age you're bound to feel burnt out or to just want to do something different by the time you're in your mid-thirties. I mean, if you start as a teenager, you're pretty much going for twenty years. At some point, you have to stop and reassess if things are really working for you. And to be quite honest, you may experience some setbacks like I did and ask yourself, is this worth fighting for? You have to ask yourself is this making me happy? Is this fulfilling me? Is this making me the best version of myself? If the answer is no to those questions, then you have make some changes.

And that's exactly what I did, I didn't let the unknown scare me anymore. I embraced it and all of its challenges so that I could live MY life exactly the way I always wanted to live it. I surrendered to the fact that you can't control and plan everything. Instead, you have to have a vision, follow your intuition and move and pivot accordingly. Also, you have to believe that you truly can do anything you want to do in this life. You may fall flat on your face, but I guarantee you that you will have learned a valuable lesson in that fall. You just have to risk getting a little bumped and bruised, and if that just so happens to happen, remember those wounds will heal and you'll be just fine. Trust the universe to reveal and deliver it all while you just enjoy that beautiful yet bumpy roller coaster ride!

I know there's a saying "happy wife, happy life" but I like to think of it as a happy woman, happy life.

It's time to Boss Up!

How can you push through the fear?

What can you learn from your fear?

What have you overcome in the past that you were fearful of?

Boss Notes

What did you learn most from this chapter?

"We delight in the beauty of the butterfly but rarely admit the changes it has gone through to achieve that beauty."
Maya Angelou

CHAPTER FOUR
Personal Development

Finding your passion isn't always easy. For example, I thought that I wanted to be a make-up artist, but I sat on this idea for a year or two and never made that commitment. I now know that I didn't commit to that idea because I was not willing to give up my weekends with my family (see a pattern here?) and honestly, I really just like doing makeup on myself. For me, it's therapeutic, it's what I like to do as a part of my self-care. I like watching YouTube tutorials in my spare time and look at the current fashion trends.

I decided to just embrace my love for makeup and just do it for fun and from there I

decided to buy a new camera and lighting and
started studying up on filming and editing. I was
gifted a heat press for making T-shirts and coffee
mugs and anything else I might dream up. I became
fearless in my decisions and started following my
intuition. I didn't know where all this would take
me, but I did know that closing my business was the
best decision I'd made for myself in a very, very
long time. I finally had the opportunity to just play.

This is exactly what I was missing in my
life. I was missing something that I enjoyed doing
even when I wasn't getting paid to do it. I was also
missing women who were encouraging, supporting,
inspiring, and uplifting to other women. I realized
that I had to do some personal development and as I
dove deeper I began to feel more confident, happier,
and most of all more inspired. I found other
amazing, ambitious and smart women that inspired
me.

One day in August of 2015, just as I was in
my last months of business, I stumbled upon a
Facebook post by a woman named Cara Alwill-
Leyba, a certified Master Life Coach and author.
She was holding a group coaching session for
female entrepreneurs. It was another sign, at just the
right time. She spoke about leaving her corporate
job after eight years and pursuing the life she
always wanted. Ding, Ding, Ding! She spoke my

language! I signed up, right then and there. With no doubts or fears, I followed my gut and signed up. That was the first time I'd actually invested in myself as far as personal development goes other than books. The experience was surreal, and Cara definitely spoke to my soul. She helped me to remember that those fears that had kept me paralyzed for years were just in my head as I was proceeding with the closure. It was the support I needed at that time.

My biggest take away from all the personal development work I did was to just start living the way you want right away, think it into existence, and then get to work for it. But again, it was a mindset shift and different way of thinking. I started to think about what I wanted my end result to be and work backwards. Take one step at a time. It was exactly what I always did in my life and now I had to do it again. I realized that all my biggest accomplishments were when I had an idea and then took small steps every day to get to that big picture goal.

It wasn't until I started working on my personal development that I got inspired again, and it felt amazing. When I started investing in myself and believing in myself, that's when things really began to shift. Knowing that as long as I followed my intuition, I could not go wrong, and everything would work itself out (it always does by the way) you just have to remind yourself. That was the catalyst of my new beginning and my new journey.

It became clear that I wanted to help empower other women to follow their intuition and create the life of their dreams. First thing was first: I had to start living my life my way, and then I could teach others how to do it.

I knew what lack of motivation felt like; I knew what it was like to have a business that no longer served me. I knew what it felt like to be held back from really pursuing the life I truly wanted to live. And if I was feeling like this I was sure there were other women out there feeling it too. By being an entrepreneur and business owner who truly dreaded dealing with an unfulfilled business daily, I knew you could not be happy without passion for your business. You have to wake up every day and have a smile on your face and feel good about what you are doing for a living or eventually you will become bored, depressed, and unmotivated or a combination of them all.

I wanted to help people—and women specifically –to realize that they did not have to feel trapped in a job, a business, a relationship or anything for that matter that no longer served them. I knew I could help them overcome their fears and follow their intuition in order to pursue their happiest life. All of this led me to taking the lifestyle and business coaching courses at the school Cara recommended. I became a certified life and business coach. I knew that by pursuing this path, I would not only lift myself higher, but I would be better equipped at uplifting others and coaching others in business too.

In November 2015, I had the opportunity to meet Cara in person at her book signing in South Jersey. She embraced me, complimented me and encouraged me. In December 2015 she invited me up to New York to a Soul Cycle Class and it was such an amazing experience. She didn't just write this amazing book about entrepreneurship and unlocking your happiness called *Girl Code*, she IS the epitome of *Girl Code*!

So, after wrapping up with the coaching certification program, I also realized how important self-care is. You have got to put yourself first so that you can be the best version of yourself for everyone around you. I realized self-care does not mean I am selfish. It truly means that I have to make myself a priority to feel fulfilled and then ultimately to help others.

I now know that the only way to live the life I want to live is to create it exactly as I want it. I wake up every day with gratitude, incorporating more of the things I like into my day, ending my day with gratitude and most importantly, surrounding myself with like-minded people.

My purpose daily is to transform my life into the life of my dreams. Finding my creativity again has been absolutely amazing! I am grateful to wake up in the morning and live life on my terms. I truly wake up happy. The real key is finding the right balance for you, what works for you and applying it daily! Now don't get me wrong, I'm still working on it myself, but I feel more in alignment with my life than ever before. I let go of the fear. I started believing in my choices again and my confidence came back! I undoubtedly know that I will be alright no matter what because I always have been before. That's not to say I won't make mistakes but I now choose not to dwell in them and actually look at them as lessons learned. My advice is to follow your intuition and everything else will fall into place!

We are not only women, we are mothers, we are lovers, we are fighters, we are warriors, we are wives, we are providers, we are nurtures, we are emotional and most of all we are human! We deserve love, appreciation and loyalty. Why don't we receive it? Because we are not giving it to ourselves. We have to stop expecting it from the outside world and just love ourselves; love all of our imperfections; love ourselves fully and unapologetically. We have to believe in our decisions and not second guess them. We are so much more powerful, smarter, sexier and beautiful than we give ourselves credit for. Beauty really does begin within; we are beautiful inside and out.

We all have chapters of our life. Some chapters are exciting. Some are sad. Some are fun. And some are downright scary. The best part is, we can always write a new chapter whenever we choose to do so. That's exactly what I've decided to do.

Like I said before, I used to be so focused on trying to be a provider and now my focus is on being a better woman. By doing that, I start with myself, by taking care of myself. If I take charge in those areas, I'll be a better person for everyone around me. We only get one life. So, make sure to do the things you want to do in order to make yourself happy. You'll then be able to help others be happy as well. Isn't the goal in life to live a happy, funny, fabulous, beautiful, sometimes sad, amazing life?

We always learn the lessons, so try not to stress about it and just be more in the everyday moments. We're all just doing the best we can.

When I decided that I was completely done with my business, did I have a nest egg? Or a safety net? Sure. Was is it enough? No. In my years of entrepreneurship, whether it's real estate, building a brick-and-mortar business, or deciding to make a transition in life, it's always going to go over budget and take double the time. It's that old Murphy's Law thing. I mean think about it: does anything really go exactly as planned? No, right? My suggestion for those who do not have it all figured out and find themselves unsure is just remember that this phase will pass. You will learn from any mistakes that are made, and honestly, I won't even call them mistakes, I would call them lessons. For everything that does not go our way a new way is formed for us, we just have to remind ourselves of that as we go through the journey of our transformation. Change is scary, man. Change is hard. If it was easy, everyone would do it. Remember that.

Going back to that Murphy's Law, when I first closed the business I knew I had my rental property and was anticipating rent from my tenants but, unfortunately, just as I closed my business, my tenants decided to stop paying rent. But you know what? I decided that it was a lesson, and that lesson was the realization that I should delegate and hire a property manager. It was in my best interest to have someone else handle the tasks of my rental property. By hiring the property manager this would take the pressure off and I would be able to focus solely on the next chapter of my life. The chapter which I like to call the most beautiful life that I could create. And what that means is I am only doing things I'm truly excited about, setting my schedule the way I want it to be, and most importantly, having creative freedom. I knew exactly what I wanted and how I want to set up my life going forward. I deep down believe that the comeback will always be greater than any setback ever was.

You just have trust your intuition and figure it out as you go! Sometimes you have to jump and hope your parachute opens along the way! It's risky, just like skydiving. You take a risk and sometimes you win, sometimes you lose but don't ever give up.

It's time to Boss Up!

If you are at a place in life and want to make changes I want, you to ask yourself some serious questions.

Are you sure this is aligned with what you really want?

What do you do when you are no longer aligned with your life as it is, a relationship or your business?

What steps can you take to get out?

What's the plan once you do make the change?

Boss Notes

What did you learn most from this chapter?

"Your work is going to fill a large part of your life, and the only way to be truly satisfied is to do what you believe is great work. And the only way to do great work is to love what you do. If you haven't found it yet, keep looking. Don't settle. As with all matters of the heart, you'll know when you find it."
Steve Jobs

CHAPTER FIVE
The Silver Lining

After I closed the business, things didn't exactly go as planned. As I stated in the previous chapter, four months after I closed, my tenant stopped paying the rent and I had to start the eviction proceedings. I wasn't counting on having to do that, actually I was counting on the rent payments to offset the loss of income from the business. The eviction process took six long months. In that six months I realized that I never wanted to be in this position again, so my husband and I decided we should hire a property manager. This would create a win-win situation. We would no longer be dealing with the day to day tasks of being landlords and I could just focus on my next business venture.

Once the tenants were evicted we had to completely renovate the house from top to bottom. As we were in the process of renovating the house someone broke in and stole all of our tools and all of the brand-new light fixtures that we purchased. Our projected availability date had to be delayed. We were so frustrated, but we kept on going.

Once we overcame that situation, we had another setback. We had a severe storm one month prior to our second projected availability date which required us to have emergency roof repairs and additional repairs to the interior work that we just renovated.

I literally had to coach myself through this whole process. I kept telling myself that everything happens for a reason. And sure enough, the real estate market went up and since we made these renovations we could now collect approximately forty percent more per month in rent payments.

I want you to know that just because things didn't work out exactly the way I thought they would, they still worked out in my favor. And I believe they always will.

In my previous business I stopped growing and progressing, I stopped coaching myself through the tough times. I stopped looking on the bright side. I was becoming complacent and that really wasn't me at the core. I was starting to lose myself. You have to allow yourself the space to evolve. After all, I had worked to get myself to this level and I deserved to give myself a break and decide what's next. I'm smart, and I believe I can start over and over again if I so chose to do so. Believe that you CAN do the thing that you may be afraid you can't do; be willing to give it a shot. That's how you know what you are truly capable of.

Having the opportunity to only focus on the investment property after going, going, going since I was a teenager felt pretty good. I was forced to only focus on one project at a time. It was almost as if the universe wanted me to slow down. This was reflection time. It was time to get reacquainted with myself.

I found that truly embracing family time is important to me. Time is something we can't get back. I've come to the realization that there is no perfect balance. I just have to move with the ebb and flow of life and business. I try to value each moment, because kids grow so fast.

I began to think deeper about having the right eating habits, workout habits, sleeping habits, etc. Not just for me but my family too.

I was so busy worrying in my previous business that I was forgetting to actually live in the moment. For example, after opening my business it took me seven years to take a vacation. I was so wrapped up in the day to day operation of the business I didn't feel like I could leave the country for a whole week. I wanted this beautifully free life, but I just didn't know how to get there or to have it all at the same time. I always felt like I had to control everything or wear too many hats in one day. Or at least I felt like I had to. Once I understood that I really couldn't control everything, my mindset shifted, and I started to live life in a more aware state.

I had appreciation for the things that didn't exactly go as I planned, because things did work themselves out. My husband received multiple raises which helped offset my loss of income and he emotionally supported me while I was in this transitional phase of entrepreneurship. All he wanted was for me to be happy. He knew how hard I worked and said, "you deserved to take some time for yourself to figure out what you want to do next."

That's when I decided that I should start a blog to document my journey as I moved from one phase of my life to another. So, I hired a graphic designer and got started on creating my little space on the Internet. Of course, this process takes time, but I realize how fun it is to go back and forth with a graphic designer and having the graphic designer taking my ideas and turning them into a reality.

Having a place to write about the process is very therapeutic for me and I realized that there are so many things I can talk about with the blogging platform. I can talk about beauty, lifestyle, DIY projects and crafting, health and wellness, my love for makeup, photography, designing, learning, business and so much more! I can collaborate with other women who have the same interests as me or can relate to my journey.

I dove into beauty because it was a way for me to deal with my anxiety. I believe makeup is a form of art and art is extremely therapeutic. As I was going through my transformational journey as an entrepreneur, I found I really enjoyed makeup, fashion, style and positivity. Combining those elements was my way of dealing with my anxiety and providing myself with a creative outlet. This is also where new my lighting, camera and editing skills would be utilized. That's how Beauty Begins Within was formed. I registered this slogan as my trademark and it would be the name of my blog. I thought this was the perfect slogan because I love makeup but ultimately, I know that working on yourself internally is much more beautiful than anything on the surface. This slogan is also carrying over into my coaching business. I coach women to believe in their intuition, the feeling deep within themselves. I want them to know that everything they are searching for is already within them. I want them to overcome any fears and anxiety about making a change in their life.

My main goal is to empower other women who may feel stuck and are afraid to make the changes that they so desperately want to make. I want to help them believe in themselves again, to trust their instincts and to go after what they truly desire. I believe that if you don't go after what you want you will live in regret. We are here to take chances and to see what happens. There's a quote "What if I fall? Oh, but darling, what if you fly?" You may fall, this is true, but like in real life, when we fall, we get right back up again. The same should go for our dreams and ideas. We should try. If we fail, it's okay just get back up and try again. There truly is no such thing as failure, there are only lessons learned.

I completely took the pressure off myself. I let my intuition lead me for a full year. I lead with my intuition and know I have this; from all the years of experience in business such as website building, brick and mortar, taxes, supply purchases, contract and lease renewals, payroll. I had all that down; now it was just time to really fall back and see where my inner guide would take me next.

So, I did just that, I gave myself time to breathe, fear would show up but now I know that is just the shadow trying to dull my true shine. It was like I was a bear in hibernation! I needed to rest to come out stronger and have a deeper desire for what I want. I came to the realization that I really was already living the life I wanted. There was just so much other noise that distracted me. I acknowledged that I needed to stop and smell the roses both literally and metaphorically. I have always been a girly girl who loves doing my makeup, getting dressed up, wearing Victoria's Secret lounge wear (when working from home), working out, reading magazines and books. I realized that I could still be an entrepreneur and be myself. I'm really just that seventeen-year-old, *Cosmopolitan* reading girl who just so happens to now be a thirty-nine-year-old mother, and wife. I'm getting back to my roots and living my life on my terms. So, my advice to you is: just Be You! You'll be so much happier, I promise!

Once I decided that I wanted to become a Life and Business Coach, that's when I knew how important a positive mindset is. I realized that personal development was an ongoing journey and not just a destination. It's where you go into each day trying to be better than you were the day before. I want to empower women, motivate women and most importantly I want to connect with women who want the same thing.

Becoming a Certified Life and Business Coach set me on a journey of self-discovery and the pursuit of my happiest life. I will no longer settle for mediocrity. I will continue to work on my personal development, my new coaching business, my new positive friendships and relationships that I've made. This is my transformation and I am determined to truly enjoy this thing called life.

My advice to you is to listen to those voices that you hear inside, those little ideas that you have but don't have the confidence to pursue. I suggest you push the fear aside and take it day by day and do a little bit every day to make the most amazing life you can. By doing this, you will feel fulfilled and when you are fulfilled you become a better woman, a better mother and a better wife. Please dream big and never stop dreaming just take it day by day and keep moving forward towards those dreams. You never know, those little ideas and those little passion projects may just become the fulfillment that you've been looking for.

I wake up every morning the way I want to. I now home school my son so we are no longer held to a particular schedule. If we want to go somewhere we schedule school around that. If we want to travel all he needs to do is bring along his laptop. We are getting to spending quality time with him. It's like I've become obsessed with improving my life in every area. I want to live a life of limitless possibilities.

I believe anything you dream you can achieve! I remember dreaming and believing that I could be successful even though I came from a very poor background. I could use my imagination for hours. I want other women to know they can do the same. The life you've imagined is waiting for you. You just have to take it step by step, day by day and most importantly have patience. It really is there for the taking.

For the past couple of years, I've been closing all of the old doors so that I could walk through the new doors fully focused and ready to help others do the same.

It's time to Boss Up!

Do you dare to dream? If so, what is your biggest dream?

Do you dare to hope, believe, feel, find, seek, receive, and to make a change?

Do you dare to fiercely pursue the life you've always imagined?

What can you start doing today to make your dream a reality?

Boss Notes

What did you learn most from this chapter?

"Where there is no struggle,
there is no strength."
Oprah Winfrey

CHAPTER SIX
Reflection

As I look back, I realize you must love yourself, love your journey, and most importantly love your life to really find happiness. Enjoy each and every moment of it. That is what is most important in life.

When things happen we always wind up learning the lessons so try not to stress about it along the way and just live in the moment. We're all doing the best we can. And as Oprah says, "When you know better, you do better."

I want you go after that thing, whatever that is to you and I want you to do it scared! Do it before you are ready! Take the leap, I know it sounds cliché, but it is SO true!

My yearning for change was because I had this undeniable desire for more peace, more moments of fun and laughter, financial freedom and more travel honestly. That's why I chose coaching. I've been through a lot and have a ton of life and business experience so why not help others with my knowledge? I didn't know how I was going to do it, I just knew I wanted to. That's just it though; it starts with a thought, then the actual vision, then the journey of taking on a new project. Just set small goals daily.

My WHY, is wanting to feel truly passionate about what I'm doing along with providing a great income and lifestyle for myself and my family. Pure joy and happiness. I want to help other women do the same thing. I want to help them overcome anxiety and fear. I want to help uplift them.

I used to set goals and have these huge expectations for myself and everyone around me. When something didn't go the way, I expected it to I would get extremely disappointed. I believe that my obsession to control things stems from my childhood when things were so out of control. Like my father's drug addiction and my parents subsequent divorce. Everything I knew was flipped upside down. However, through a lot of inner work, I have learned that I can't control things no matter how hard I try and honestly, the harder I try the unhappier I feel. I acknowledged that things are going to happen, and you can't predict the outcome. I had to learn to release my choke hold on perfection and let things unfold as they do. It took me thirty-seven years to come to this realization. Now I just control myself, my decisions, my reactions, my actions and it has changed my mindset completely.

I want to empower women to realize they can have anything they want, no matter their background. All they have to do is own that they want it. I help women realize they can have the life and business they've always dreamed of. I encourage them to dream big and show them that the life they want is attainable. I absolutely love seeing women achieve their goals and watching them create the life and businesses they have always wanted. I love seeing women transform their lives. It gives me great pleasure and satisfaction watching women reach their true potential.

I truly believe that my business superpower is my intuition! I start to listen to the voice inside. I follow my instincts and push past the fear. I am a big dreamer; a woman who believes that the possibilities are limitless! The principles that guide me and my work are passion, ambition and creativity. The biggest point that I want to make is to dream big and believe in those dreams very passionately! Everything you need is within you to succeed. You just have to remember that. Follow your intuition! Be open to even bigger things. Sometimes, we get so caught up in the HOW and we stop progressing. Just envision what you want, hold that vision and take steps each day towards that vision. There will be ups and downs but please view them as lessons. Let go of the HOW and just live in the moment. You cannot control everything! (This is something I still work on every day!)

If something doesn't go as planned, you have to feel the emotions; sit with them. Work on yourself. If you have to go to therapy to talk it out, do it, I did. I would read motivating books; journal and I even placed a positive message on refrigerator every morning for a year. Every time I'd go into my kitchen I would read that message. Acknowledge all that has happened. And then learn to channel that energy in a positive way. Detach from your past, you aren't going that way.

Come from a place of love with yourself. Don't say mean things to yourself. Say, "I can do this to improve myself or this situation."

You have to tear down the house metaphorically speaking and rebuild a brand-new foundation! It can be scary but if you want a new life you have to destroy or release the old one! It's like you literally have to flip your whole life upside down. Start building your new one, one day at a time. One step after another. Don't look at the whole picture or all the steps you need to take at one time because that will surely cause overwhelm and just stress you out. Just take action every day in a positive direction.

When my life called me to be more still than I was ever comfortable with in the past, gratitude is what got me through. Gratitude for the opportunity I had created; the opportunity to take a year off and actually feel, comprehend, appreciate, and breathe.

Don't get me wrong. When you are going through a transformational time in your life, you may have days where you question everything, and fear will creep in. You may wonder if you made the right decision or could you have handled things differently? Stop those thoughts in their tracks and think of all the positive in your life, think of all your previous accomplishments you've had.

Also remember, just because your plan may get off course doesn't mean it's wrong. Maybe it's just redirection. I like to believe the universe is guiding me and I'm intuitively following.

People tried to break me, people have robbed me, people intentionally set out to hurt me, and I realized they really don't have that kind of power. That power is mine and I choose to rise above just like I always have. I have always risen, and I always will. I have had setbacks and I've had heartache, but nothing will stop me from getting back up and completing my goals. I've lit that match and burned those bridges, so I never ever go back.

Entrepreneurship can be hard. It can be lonely and isolating. It has its ups and it has its downs, but you have to remain strong and keep fighting and keep believing that everything will work out just as it should. I'm not saying that I don't have days where I break down and cry because honestly, I do. I'm only human, but I get back up, face whatever setback has come my way and move forward.

You will have people come for you. I have literally had people set out intentionally to hurt me and my family out of pure hate and vengeance. As a landlord, I've had to evict people. Those people were even considered "friends" and "family." They went as far as to squat in my home, destroy and intentionally vandalize the home all because I could no longer allow them to live there for free.

See the thing with some people is that they don't know the value of a dollar. All they see are the things that you have. Just because you own multiple homes doesn't mean you don't have mortgages that need to be paid. For every luxury that you have, you worked for that luxury. And just because you were a supposed "friend", or you were a "family" member does not mean you get to live off of my dollar or my hard work. You must take a stand as an entrepreneur, you must protect your business and your family, and you must be willing to stand alone. Like I said, people will test you and you will lose a lot along the way, but just know and remember those people weren't meant to come along with you as you move upward and onward. I'm not going to say it doesn't hurt because it does. It really does. But you must also realize that it is a huge blessing too.

When you are successful there are people out there that want what you have. They will try to do whatever they can do take you down with them for their own personal gain. They will sue you just to get a piece of what you have.

Being an entrepreneur isn't easy. There is no such thing as an overnight success. If you ask the people that are successful they will tell you they've been at it for years and years. They didn't just wake up one day, come up with an idea and then the money just started pouring in. That's just not how it works. If you ask them, they will tell you: they had struggles, they've had things that didn't go their way, they've had people turn their back on them, they've heard the answer "no" a lot. But the thing is, they were persistent. They did not give up when they heard the answer "no." They redirected themselves and figured out a new way. They took the lessons they learned from what some would say "failures" and moved along pushing forward. That's what successful people do, that's what hustlers do, that's what people who have great desires and ambition do. They push forward, plain and simple. That really is the answer: keep on moving. Now, I'm not saying you don't take time out to feel a little sorry for yourself because honestly sometimes you do really have to feel the feels. Sometimes you have to take a moment to process what's going on, process what just happened, and then pick yourself up and move on. When those people tried to mentally break me, I thought I wanted revenge, but something came over me. It was pity. I realized how utterly miserable they had to be to desperately try to hurt me and take me down. Being at peace and truly happy was the best revenge I could ever seek. Not just for myself but my family too! I remember the "friend" I fired saying "it's not going to end the way you think it is", and she was right, it turned out so much better!

When money is involved even your friends can become your enemies. It's sad, man. I feel sorry for anyone that has envy or jealousy to that degree in their heart. If someone is spreading false rumors, slandering you, or trying to destroy your life purposefully, remember it says everything about them and absolutely nothing about you. Please keep this message in your heart, it gets better because you are better.

What I've learned is that it truly takes a sad person to set out to hurt you and tear you down. I have been a victim of this and to be honest, I don't even like to use the word "victim" because I really became victorious. I actually feel really sorry for anyone who has to live their life that way. And I've also realized that a person who acts that way has no real purpose, peace or happiness in their life. So just remember if someone is purposely trying to hurt you, it's a reflection of who they are, not you. Keep being you, hold your head high and release any and all negativity from your life. You deserve it, beautiful!

Take those bricks that were thrown at you and build yourself a brand-new foundation!

It's time to Boss Up!

How do you find your passion? Start by incorporating some of these things into your daily life and watch how things start to shift for you.

1. Find a hobby.

2. Get out of your head. Don't let doubts or insecurities sideline you.

3. Be active. It just makes you feel better all around.

4. Take risks.

5. Try something new.

Boss Notes

What did you learn most from this chapter?

"I didn't really know what I wanted to do, but I knew the woman I wanted to become."
Diane Von Furstenberg

CHAPTER SEVEN
Patience

Both Perspective and Patience begin within us. When you are going through a transitional time in your life, that's when you realize who you really are. It's like you open layer after layer of yourself. You are evolving and growing like the bloom of a beautiful rose.

I've been aggressively trying to be a better version of myself over the past couple of years. At this point in my life I have been sued, I have been attacked by bullies and Internet thugs. I've been stolen from, taken advantage of, and everything else. You get the point. I literally had to fight for what was right. I've been redefining, reassessing and restructuring my life my way and on my terms.

I cut the bullshit friendships out of my life and the people that brought the bullshit into my life. Once you go through some tough stuff you gain wisdom and spot the bullshit and manipulation a mile away. I just get this gut feeling. If the vibe isn't right I walk away. I lit that match and watched my old life burn. I literally and metaphorically bet the motherfucking house on the pursuit of my happiness and a life that I am proud to live and that I'm excited about every day! I literally turned every lesson learned into a pot of gold!

See, in my twenties I thought that I could take everyone along with me or I could help others that came from the same place as I did. I thought that if they just had a chance they could be so good, and they could do so good. But that's the thing, people have to want it for themselves. I've learned that they have to do it, they half to want it for themselves bad enough, you cannot, and I mean you cannot do it for them. It's like when you're doing good, you feel like you want to give everyone a chance. I learned that you can't, you just can't. Not everyone is ready or equipped for that chance. And when you change not everyone changes with you.

I had another situation where I would have friends and family coming to me and telling me things and I didn't actually listen to the gossip, but I did start to pay attention to the behavior and when the behavior started to match exactly what the people were telling me, I knew. There just comes a time in your life where you know you can no longer help people just to help people. You have to help people that want to be helped.

As I stated in the previous chapter, I had tenants in my rental property and for the first year or, so it was alright but then again, I started hearing that there may be some drug use going on. Then, the rent payments stop coming in and I had to decide once again to put my family first. I had to go through the eviction process and then after I evicted the tenants, they had the nerve to break back into my home. Now, prior to evicting these tenants, I contacted their family members for help in the matter. They didn't help. So, what was I left to do?

They had now become evicted and then they broke back into the house—and destroyed it. The carpets were disgusting, the air conditioning unit was literally pulled out leaving a whole in the wall exposing the outside. I assume they were trying to get some copper out of it, I'm not sure but what I do know is my house was a complete disaster. They even pulled the electrical meter off, so they could steal electricity. It was terrible. So, I decided that I needed to call the police and have them physically removed from the premises. They were arrested for trespassing. Did I want to have to do that?

Absolutely not. But I thought maybe this would be a wakeup call for them and to their family members to help or get them help.

Needless to say, I didn't show up to court to pursue the charges against them because I didn't want to throw these people in jail. Jail is not where these people need to be, they need help in other ways. I guess why I go on to say all this is that it wasn't until my thirties that I realized that I could not help others, I could only be the leader of my immediate family and help those who want to be helped.

I cannot allow others to drag me and my family down with them and they tried, believe me they tried and when I say they tried I mean maliciously tried. But my point here is I finally realized that I have a husband, two children and now even a grandchild. These are the people that are worthy of my help. These are the people that I love and care about dearly and I will protect them against any person who tries to callously attack our family. Whether it's verbally, physically or just plain old going after our assets and money. I did not work from the age of thirteen to thirty-nine to allow other people's problems to come into my life and take from me time and time again. I was done with that life. So, I began to build a new one. I now know that I am hard as nails yet soft as silk; it's just that your attitude and your actions will dictate which side you see.

You have to take the good with the bad. You are here on this earth to challenge yourself. You have to take chances even if they don't go as well as you wanted them to go. Defeat is not failure. You are just being redirected or shifted or taught something but definitely don't look at it as failure. What I'm trying to say is always and I mean always look for the silver lining; you may not recognize it right away, however, I promise you will eventually! If you stop taking chances, then what are you going to do? You'll be stagnant; you won't be learning, and you won't be growing. Literally taking chances has been a way of life for me and I won't stop now. I don't believe in placing all your eggs in one basket either. I think you should have several baskets. Just as you would invest your money; invest yourself and your time in multiple baskets.

One thing that I truly believe that entrepreneurs have in common is this intuitive sense. They trust the gut feelings that they get and move with it. And they're also a little crazy and it's the kind of crazy where we are seriously crazy enough to believe that we can do anything! And honestly, I personally don't see it as crazy but people on the outside look at us like we are. I think that's just their fear, maybe they are afraid for us. I don't think it comes from a malicious place, they may just be scared to take risks themselves.

It's okay. I'm alright with being this type of crazy and I hope you are too! And one thing that won't change is their ambition based off of someone's judgment or perception of their endeavors. Entrepreneurs continue; they push forward no matter what. They don't just stop what they are doing because someone doesn't understand it. They show them what they can do. It's okay that not everyone has the same vision. Don't resist that, embrace it.

Always be a beginner and that's how you become a master. It takes years and years to become a master but what people don't see are all the years you were a beginner. I love being the beginner that's the exciting part; it's like having no idea how you're going to do something and then you just have to figure it out. That process is just beautiful to me. It inspires, motivates and excites me! When I'm talking about a new project, my husband says that's when I light up. Also, I've noticed that most entrepreneurs have this innate sense of gratitude. They are truly grateful for everything they go through both the ups and the downs. Now, isn't that amazing?

I remember when I first started my brick-and-mortar business. I did everything from my two-story row home in Philadelphia. Where the living room and dining room were connected. And I would work from the computer which was a couple feet away from the living room area where the TV and the couch were. My kids were young, I'd work my day job and then I'd find time in between to work on my business. Now here I am in my single-family home with my own office. I have worked hard and overcome a lot to get here. It took me years.

People go through stuff and things happen, but ultimately, it's how you recover that defines you and your character and it shows you exactly what you're made of and how mentally strong you really are.

When you are an entrepreneur at times you have to make a decision in a moment's notice. A decision that may not just affect you but those who work for you, their families, your family, etc. It can feel heavy at times and you just have to believe that the decision you made was the best that you could've made at that time. And if I'm being really real it's not easy. Sometimes, it's downright hard and sometimes you just want to cry and hope that the decision you made was the right one. On the flipside, just know that you can't really make a mistake, because even mistakes are learning lessons. I believe that no matter what everything will work itself out. As the old saying goes "big risks equal big rewards".

If I can convince you of anything, I hope it is that there are no failures, only lessons learned. Embrace those lessons! They will be used for the next decision, project or business idea. This version of me has been decades in the making. I also kind of realize that in life sometimes things have to completely fall apart in order for better things to come together in your favor. I definitely believe that to be true. It's a journey. It's a roller coaster ride. There is no easy way and there are no shortcuts.

I feel like it's my duty as an entrepreneur to let people know about the losses too. Being an entrepreneur is not as glamorous as it looks; you really have to work at it. Most entrepreneurs are just showing the highlight reel and my goal here is to let you know there are dark periods as well. However, I want you to know that you will overcome them.

You should embrace the space you're in. It's hard starting over and changing things up. If you have to take time away from others and really focus on yourself, do so. If you feel like you are starting to feel isolated, then find like-minded individuals and connect with them. Facebook groups are amazing for finding like-minded people.

I am no longer driven by having to provide for my family, it's purely based and fueled by how I want my best life to be. I've been carefully curating the life that feels truly authentic to me. I look at it like this, I'm a student again. I learn, I study, I test, and I balance family life the best I can. I have my head down, minding my "business" and keeping my circle tight. That's just really the bottom line.

Don't call it a comeback because I never even went anywhere. I've just been rediscovering myself as female entrepreneur. And now I'm ready to help other women do the same.

It's time to Boss Up!

Here are some boss tips I want to share with you.

1.   Be careful of the people you allow into your life.

2.   Set solid boundaries.

3.   Fearlessly release toxic people from your life whenever you feel the need to.

Boss Notes

What did you learn most from this chapter?

"I feel there are two people inside me – me and my intuition. If I go against her, she'll screw me every time, and if I follow her, we get along quite nicely."
Kim Basinger

CHAPTER EIGHT
Owning your Intuition

I guess why I'm writing this book is to let you know that it's alright to change your mind at any given time. If something is no longer working for you, it's no longer making you feel good, or you're no longer excited about doing it, it is 100% OK to admit it and change it up.

I also know as we get older and we have more responsibilities like mortgages, children, car payments, and the like, it's so scary or can appear to be super scary to make a change but isn't staying in an unhappy situation scarier? It was for me.

Most importantly, I really want to drive home the importance of listening to your intuition.

You know deep down. You already know what the answers are because they are within you. I'm not going to say that you won't struggle when you make a decision to change because change is never easy, and I want to make that very clear as well. However, what I do know is living a couple years a little uncomfortably to change things about your life or business is worth it in the end. You may not see it while you're in the eye of the storm of this transformation, but you will see it once the storm passes and the transition is made.

I also want you to know, that your intuition is like a muscle. The more you use it and own it, the more comfortable you get with your decision-making. You decide what is working for you and what is not. You stop asking the people around you what they think, and you just go for it. As an entrepreneur, you have to be able to think fast and make decisions quickly. When situations like this come up follow what feels good to you and your intuition. That's owning it!

If you sit and think back on your life up to this point, like many people, you have probably faced more and have done more then you could have ever imagined. You have probably already overcome so much in your life and you got through it all by making decision after decision and following your intuition. I know I have many experiences. I am both a high school dropout and a college graduate. I have rented apartments and purchased homes. I've taken public transportation and purchased cars. As a kid I dreamt of vacations and as an adult have had my passport stamped. There is such beauty in knowing both worlds.

I always knew I was destined for more, more of what? I wasn't quite sure, I just knew it was more than the place I started, or the area I was raised. I knew one day my story would help people; it would touch them in some way. I'm grateful to finally share my story of both success and lessons learned.

It is through your decisions and subsequent obligations that you have had to flex and build your boss like intuitive muscle. Some of the most difficult experiences and their valuable lessons are what got us to this beautiful point in our lives. It all begins within you. You just have to tap into it, you know what you need to do. So, boss up, beautiful!

In my opinion, the best thing about being an entrepreneur is the comfort in knowing that you're in control of you own destiny with each and every decision that you make. You are literally the creator of your life, and that's just beautiful.

Having gratitude is also imperative. Showing gratitude for everything and every situation that has happened in your life shows that you have great faith in what is to come. When you have gratitude and you're following your intuition that's the real key to transforming your life. You should be thankful for every lesson and grateful for your powerful intuition.

Your intuition is such a beautiful tool and, yet, we often push it away. And of course, in hindsight you're thinking: *damn, I knew that wasn't right.* So, when a situation comes up, I want you to step away from everyone, don't ask everyone else for their opinion, and just sit alone with your thoughts. You have the answers within, you always have, and you always will.

Our intuition is really just all about our instincts and our feelings. As I laid everything out earlier in this book, most of my decision were based on my beliefs. I have to provide. I have something to prove. How does this affect my family? See? Very analytical. It wasn't until I stopped, got quiet and listened to myself, my intuition that I became a happier version of myself. I looked back and realized, damn girl, I've had the answers all along. I always will. And you do too!

Follow your intuition, no matter what. Don't be afraid of the judgment of your peers, your friends, your parents, or relatives. They aren't the ones living your life, and they most certainly aren't the ones who see your vision. So, don't for a second let anyone's opinion distract you from obtaining your happiness. Follow your instincts and dive into creating your biggest, boldest, and most beautiful life. I promise, you won't regret it, not even a little bit! You don't want to look back on your life and think I should have. You'll want to look back and say I'm glad that I tried or I'm glad I did. If you ask someone older if they have any regrets in life most often they will tell you that they regret the things they didn't do, not the things they did do.

I also want women to know that it's alright to still want to feel beautiful inside and out. Life is not over as you approach forty. I want you to know that you can be any age and still enjoy feeling beautiful, stylish, glamorous, be business savvy, and also be a mother and a wife. There's total femininity at any age. I realize as I approach forty that this is just the beginning and I'm embracing that! I want you to embrace it also! Believe you can do anything you want, at any age and you will.

The best thing you can do for yourself is to love yourself, be yourself and shine like a boss among the ones who doubted your ability. The minute you stop caring about what others think and start doing what you really want to do is when you will know true freedom. Do yourself a favor and don't ever hide your power. Don't water yourself down to protect another person's ego or insecurities.

Focus your energy on creating a positive life for yourself. And once you awaken and focus that positive energy, a brand-new life unfolds before your very eyes. When you learn to walk alone, it can be hard, but that walk is the walk that makes you the beautiful boss that you are.

I know that blindly trusting your intuition and yourself may seem easier said than done, but it is a necessary step to living your most beautiful life. It's a boss move and a powerful one at that!

So, go out there and Boss Up, Beautiful!

It's time to Boss Up!

Here are some boss tips I want to share with you.

Love yourself and every decision you have made. There is no wrong way.

Continue to challenge yourself because it helps you grow.

Raise your expectations in business and life. By raising your expectation people will either rise with you or they won't. Either way everything will work itself out.

Boss Notes

What did you learn most from this chapter?

ACKNOWLEDGEMENTS

To my husband Mike for always loving me and believing in me no matter what. To my mom for always supporting me. To my children, Michael and Logan, you are my heart and soul, you give me strength every day. To my grandson Gavin for always filling our house with laughter whenever you come to visit. To my sister-in-law Mickey for listening to me, laughing with me and sometimes even crying with me. I love you all so much. I am truly grateful to have each one of you in my life. Thank you, thank you, thank you!